LONDON
Through A Lens

For Em, Molly, Mum & Dad, Liz, Tilly, Bobo & To All At Syon

For London & Flickr

For Alan

And For Me

Southwark Underground

INTRODUCTION

To put it simply, I love London with a deep passion. It is she who has given me this opportunity to release my third book devoted to the city I adore.

When out photographing London's city streets I always try and remember to look up—a lot of my best inspiration comes from exposing eye catching angles, clean lines, architectural design and subtle human elements; standing out as unique in a city photographed by the masses

It is in post-production where the photos come alive as I experiment with different techniques to create stunning illusions.

It is truly a dream pastime to be driven around the city, hanging out of the window with camera in hand, snapping away at secret moments and landscapes hidden within the bustling city streets, whether they be the skyscrapers and waterfronts of Canary Wharf or the ever developing new urban sprawl.

London is an ever changing city, blink and one building disappears and another one appears bigger, taller and shinier. London has past, present and future; an essence of class, style, diversity, culture, tradition, beauty, classicality, cosmopolitanism and life. This is a collection of photos of now, this moment in time. In ten years from now, how many of these photos will be the same? This is a photographic moment, a vision of the here and now in London and you are invited in to share the moment as seen through a new eye.

Allow this book to transport you to the exciting, bustling streets of London from the comfort of your home. Imagine yourself strolling the streets at night watching the lights blur and the world roll by. Buildings are twisted and contorted, landscapes manipulated; all to create a dynamic new look that will change the way you see one of the greatest cities in the world.

Simon Hadleigh-Sparks is an award-winning photographer who has been the recipient of multiple international awards and recent successes include Winner in 2015 Urban Photographer Of The Year, Winner and Best in Show at the 2014 London Photo Festival, Highly Commended in the 2014 Urban Photographer of the Year, and 3rd place in the Monochrome category of the 2014 International Garden Photographer of the Year Awards as well as Highly Commended in Best Garden category. He also had various works exhibited in 2013/2014/2015 in and around London. His photos can currently be seen on a number of websites, blogs and magazine articles.

Photography starts with the push of the shutter button, but it doesn't end there; it never has and it never will.

River Thames

Our City – London by Simon & His Camera

Skyline Supremacy

Smooth London Nights

Thames Trips – Canary Wharf & O2

Canary Wharf Underground

Never Dull – Trafalgar Square

Look Out Over Our City – London

Look Out Over Our City | London

Look Out Over Our City – London

Neon Blended – Westminster City

Two Towers – Tower Bridge & The Shard (Night)

Victorian London

Westminster & The Thames

London's Disneyland – St James's Park

Buckingham Palace – St James's Park

Summer Hazy Days – London Skyline

The Icon – Tower Bridge

HMS Belfast & The Towers on River Thames

*Looking Across Thames to the North side
— LA Noir London Abstract Noir*

Crossing The Millenium Bridge

The London Look – London Silhouette

The City From Greenwich

At The Setting Of The Sun

Beauty In The Eye Of The Beholder – St George Wharf

Clapham Underground London

Towards The Tower

Foster's Crossrail Place Roof Garden – Canary Wharf

Never Negative – London City

London Pink Evening

The Dome – O2 Arena

*Keep On Building Higher Until
Theres No More Room Up There*

True Blue & Patriotic

Palace Cleaner

London Red Eye – Chinese New Year

Hampton Court Palace Summer Days

Depth of Feeling – From Millennium Bridge

Celebrations

Second Busiest In London — Canary Wharf Underground

Going Home – Waterloo Bridge

Night Lights Again – Tower Bridge

Emirates Air Cable Car & Excel Docklands

Horse Guards Parade From River

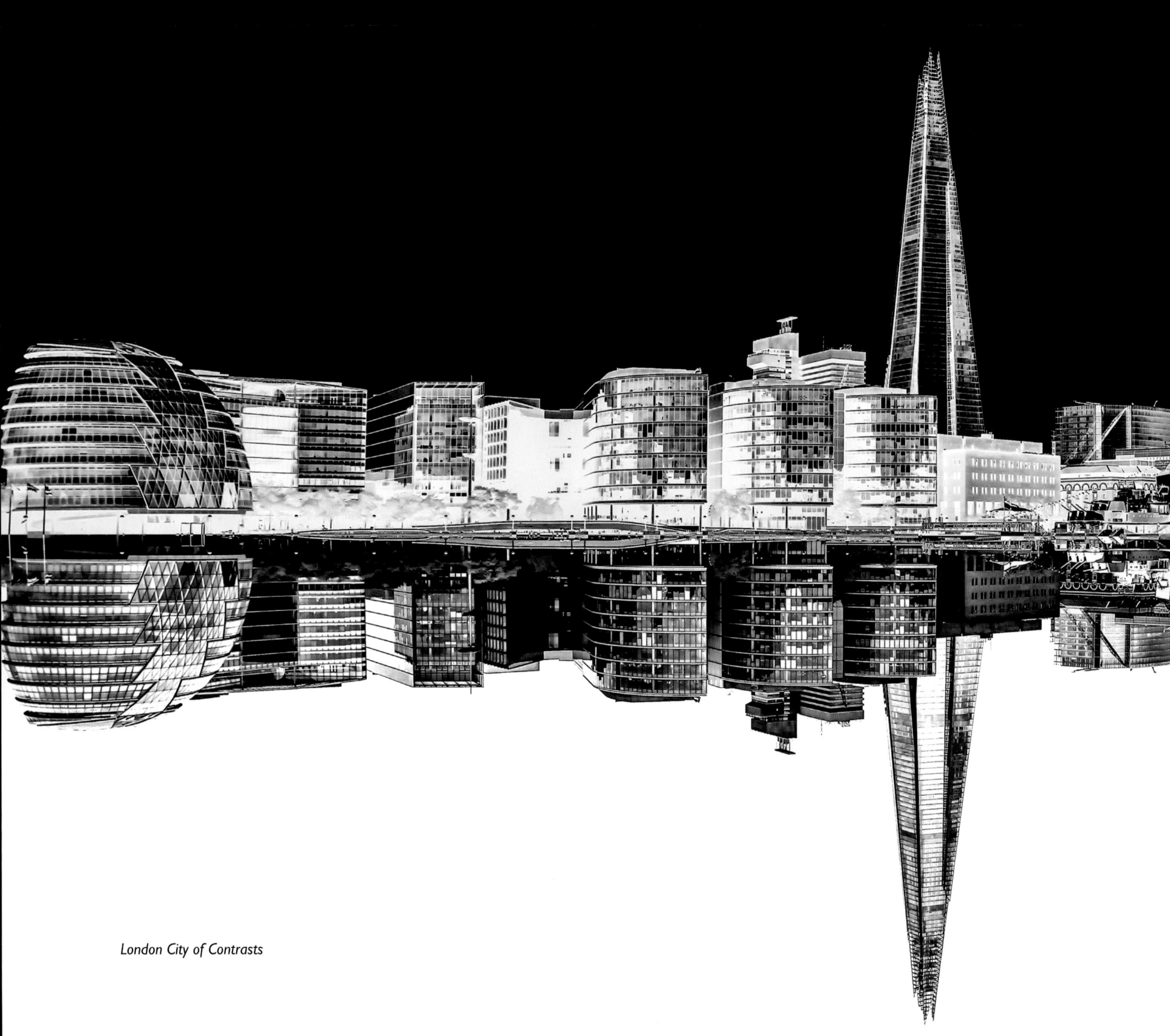
London City of Contrasts

London City Triangle

More London Reflected

More London Riverside

Queen Elizabeth Olympic Park (River Lea)

Queen Elizabeth Olympic Park (River Lea)

Queen Elizabeth Olympic Park

Symmetric Mall

Battersea Park

Skywalk

Millenium Bridge & Tate Modern

Red White & Blue In London City

The Evening Shard London

Still Pond – Richmond Park

Turner's View – Richmond Hill

Urban City London

What A View London (Olympic Park Aquatic Centre)

The Savage Curtain – Lloyds Building Reflected

The Freedom To Make My Own Mistakes Was All I Ever Wanted

Admiralty Arch

Metal & Glass London City Evolves – Broadgate

Little Venice

We Can Do Tonight Again – London City

More London Horizon

*Street Boats –
Albert Embankement*

The London Cable Cars – The Emirates Air Line

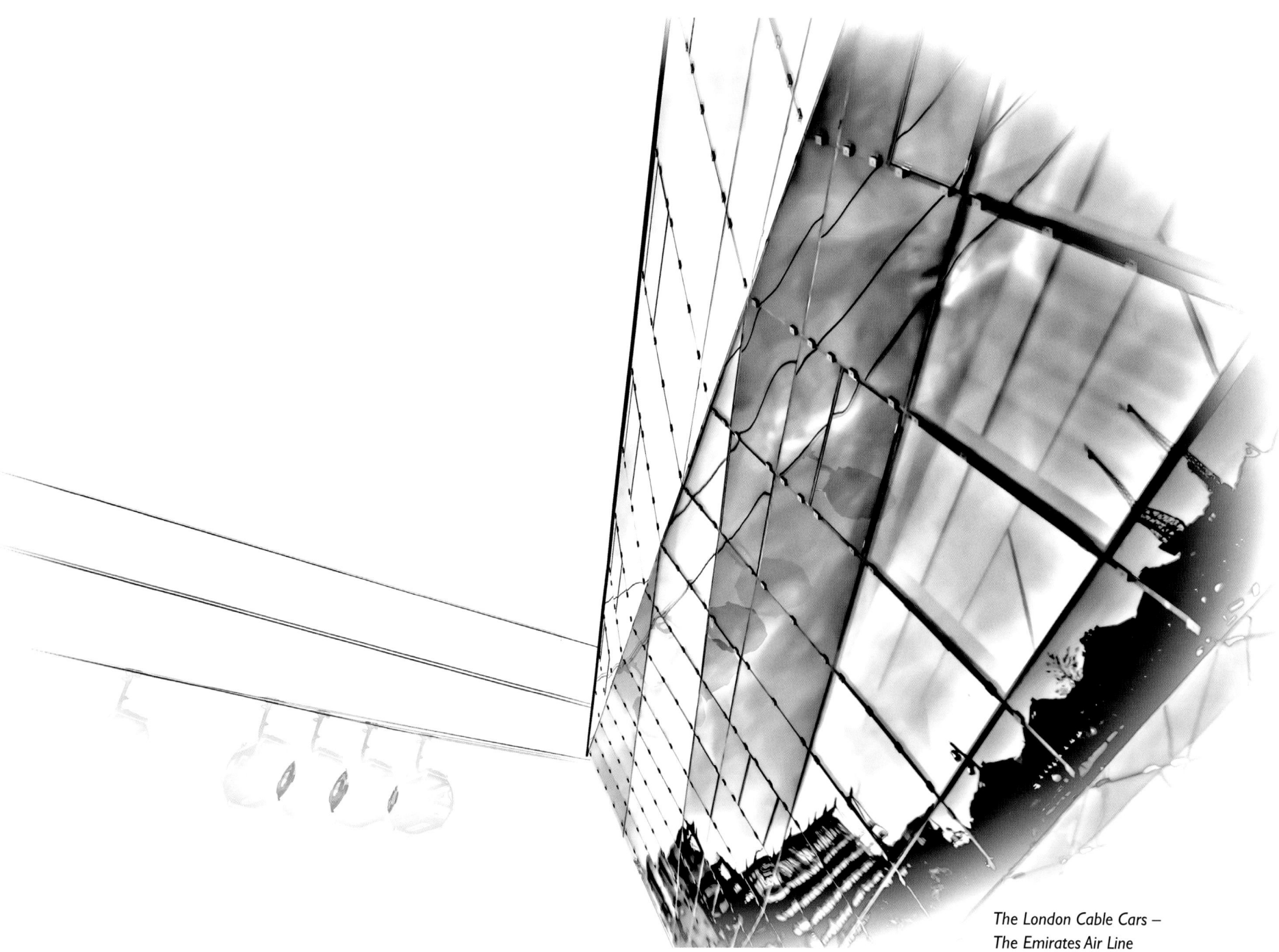

*The London Cable Cars –
The Emirates Air Line*

Across The City

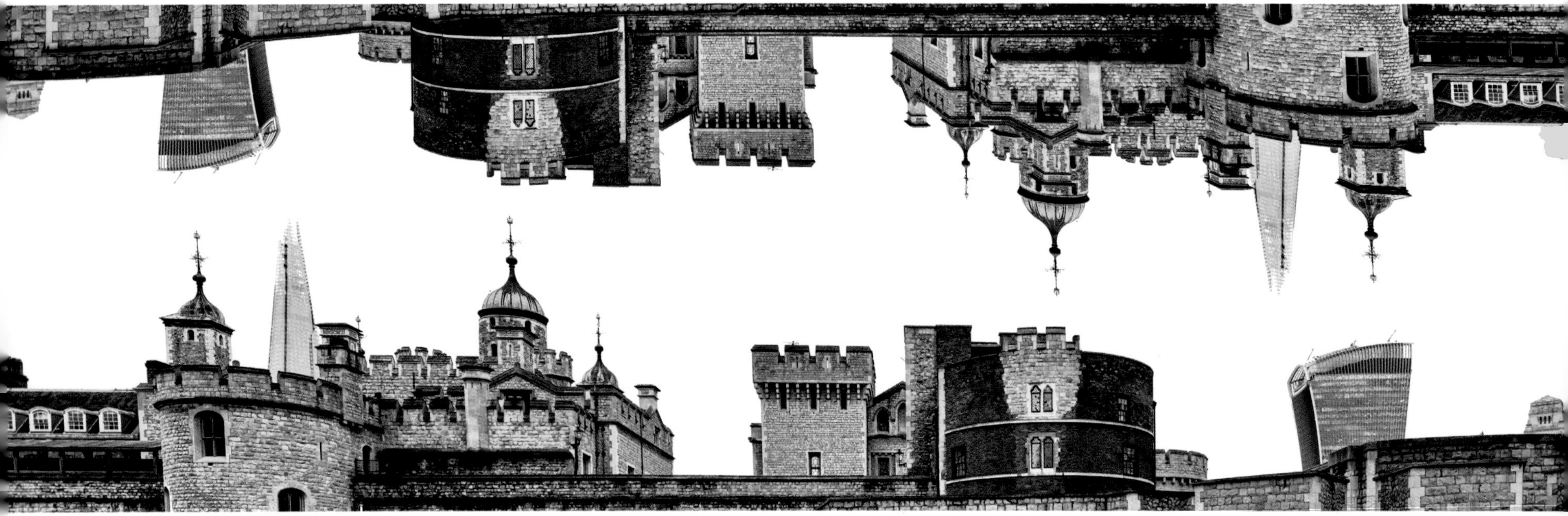

When Two Worlds Collide – City Past & Future

Freedom Is Fleeting

Hampton Court Palace

Hampton Court Palace & Flower Show

Hampton Court Long Water

Skyline Winter Morning

Skyline Summer Bright Days

London Time For Change

London Two Towers

Medusa – London City Hall

Neon Westminster London City

Old Royal Naval College Greenwich

Pushed Right To The Edge

Sicilian Avenue Holborn

*St Katharine Docks &
The Dicken's Inn*

Syon House Front Lawn – Frosty Sunrise

'I May Bite' – Horse Guards

On & Above – The Thames

Kennington Underground

On & Above – The Thames

Kennington Underground

London Garden City – Canary Wharf

Terminal 5 Underground Heathrow

The Spike – O2 Arena (London Architecture)

The Sun – Wake Up World (Syon Park Thames Floodplain)

Urban Jungle

Winter Sunset - Start Of Something New (Syon Park)

*This Is My Neverending Story –
Millwall Dock*

Morning Boat Ride – Canary Wharf

*Out Of The Office Window –
View From The Shard*

Four Bridges & The Curve

Three Blackfriars Bridges

Vision Of The Glass Shard

Sanctuary – London City

One Sunset Two Minutes – Over The Thames

Wish Less – Cubitt Town

Eyes On London

After Freedom – London City Office Life

Rainbow UFO – The Gherkin

Living High in London

Tower Bridge

London Hypothetical Impression

Moment In Eden

Autumn Years – The Path Becomes Uncertain – Abney Park

Autumn Years – The Path Becomes Uncertain – Abney Park

Red Balloon – Syon Park

Sunset Silhouette Syon Park

City Of Dreams – St James Park

A Different Age – Syon House South Side

Isabella Plantation Richmond Park

London City Dreamscape

Landscape Mirage – Syon Park

Frosty Sunrise – Syon House & Thames

The Thames Sunrise – Syon House Rear

Syon Park Floodplain Across Thames – Winter Landscape

The Wyatt Bridge Syon Park

Sunrise Over Syon House

Winter Morning – Syon Park Gardens & The Great Conservatory

Syon Park – Capability Brown Landscape

Welcome To My Planet – Syon Park

Syon Park Gardens Winter Sunrise

Reflecting On Another Time – Syon House

Syon House Turn Out The Lights – Evening Sunset

Syon Park – The Lodges & Front Lawn

England's Green & Pleasant Land – Syon House Gardens

England's Green & Pleasant Land – Syon House Gardens

Syon House & Lodges London

Syon House Brentford

Dippy The Dinosaur – Natural History Museum

United – Queen's Jubilee Flag Southbank

Between Terminal

There Are Days Like This In London City

Another Bank Underground

Popular DLR Station Tunnel

Terminal 1 Underground Walkway Heathrow

Terminal 3 Underground Heathrow

Terminal 5 Underground Walkway Heathrow

Terminal 5

Into Madness – London City Life (King's Cross)

Spring Into Autumn – Canary Wharf

Eye & Ben Trilogy

St Katharine Docks

St Katharine Docks & Real Tower Bridge Hotel

St Katharine Docks

Arrival Into The New World

My Little Planet – Syon Park Gardens – The Great Conservatory

Nature Within – Canary Wharf Office

Between A Rock & A Hard Place –
Old Broad Street

Vertical Imitation – Blackfriars Road

Buildings Can Be Sexy – London Wall

City On The Edge Of Forever – Angel Lane Bankside

Nail In The City – Cheapside

Construction – Blackfriars Road

Mirror Mirror – New Street Square

The Monolith – National Police Memorial The Mall

Return To Tomorrow – Tower Hill

Stealth – Euston Road

Stop The World I Want To Get Off – Bankside

Tetris Office – Paddington Basin

Sweet Logic – Tower Hill

Paint Reflections Of Me In Their Eyes

Tower Bridge Opens

Tower of London

The Shard Under Millennium Bridge

The Glass Shard

The Trafalgar Lions

The Thames Sphinx

The Stare

All Roads Lead To London

Moorgate Underground London

King's Cross Underground London

Leicester Square Underground London

Bank Underground London (Waterloo & City)

Green Park Underground London

St Johns Wood Underground London

Keep Left – Bank Underground London (Waterloo & City)

King's Cross Underground London

King's Cross Underground London

King's Cross Underground London

Leicester Square Underground London

Embankment Underground London

The Face Of The City 'Iron' – London

The Face Of The City 'Liquid' – London

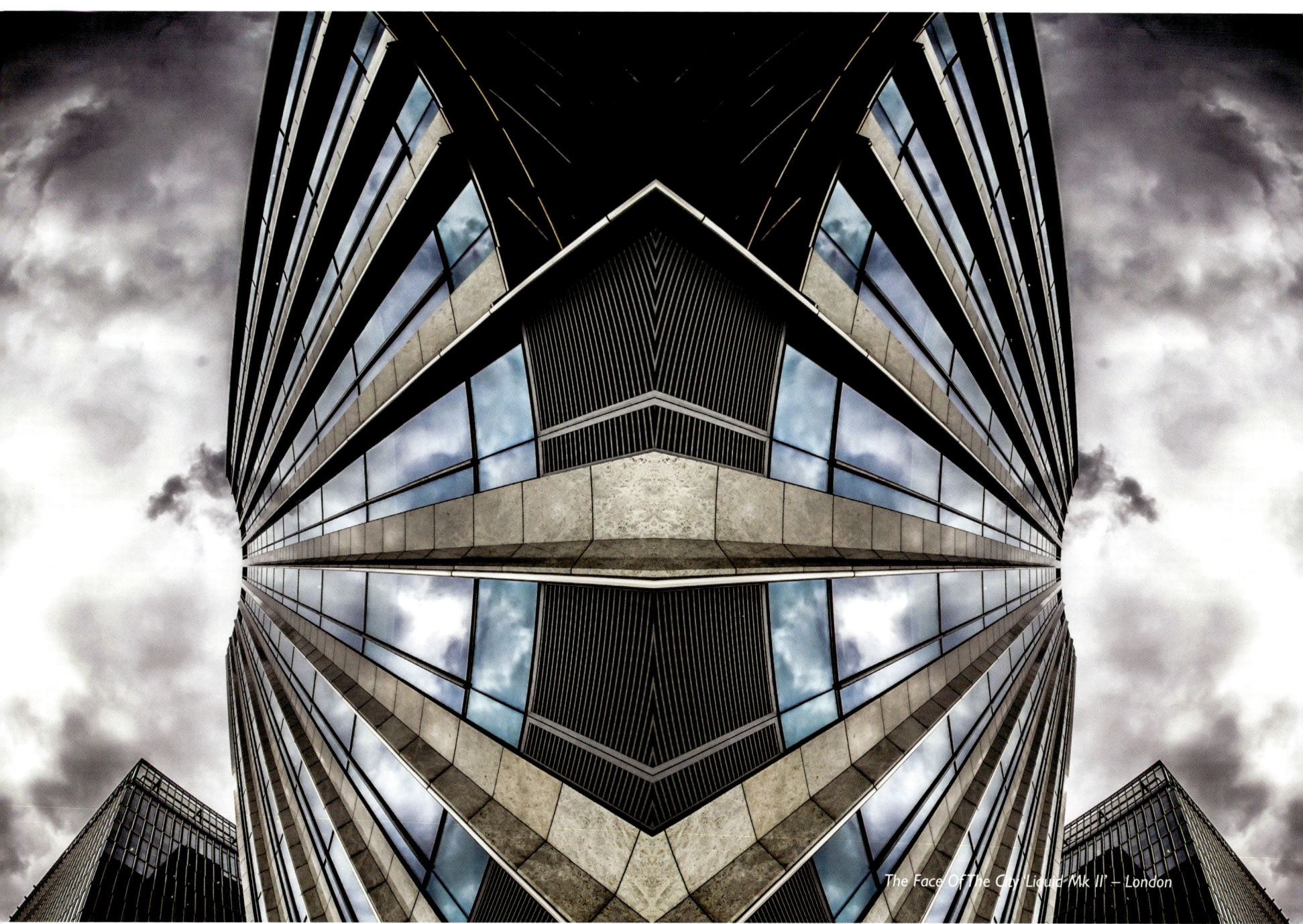

The Face Of The City 'Liquid Mk II' – London

The Face Of The City 'Olympic' – London

Natural History London

True Blue My World - London City Office Life

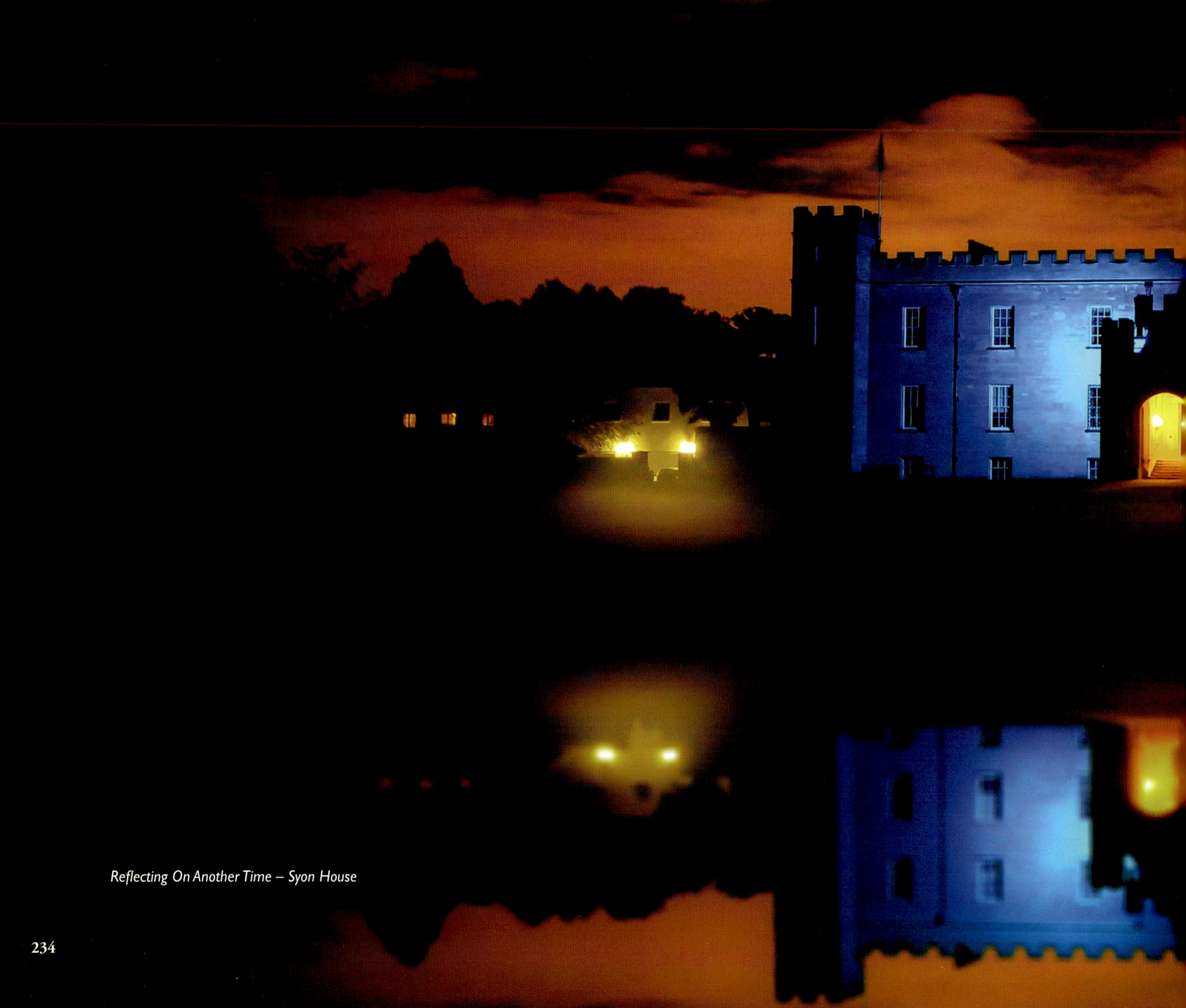

Reflecting On Another Time – Syon House

Syon House – The Great Conservatory Summer

Syon Park Gardens – The Great Conservatory

Syon Park Gardens London Enchanted Woodland

Syon Park Gardens London Enchanted Woodland

First published in 2016 by New Holland Publishers Pty Ltd
London • Sydney • Auckland

The Chandlery Unit 009 50 Westminster Bridge Road London SE1 7QY United Kingdom
1/66 Gibbes Street Chatswood NSW 2067 Australia
5/39 Woodside Ave Northcote, Auckland 0627 New Zealand

www.newhollandpublishers.com

Copyright © 2016 New Holland Publishers Pty Ltd
Copyright © 2016 in text: Simon Hadleigh-Sparks
Copyright © 2016 in images: Simon Hadleigh-Sparks

All rights reserved. No part of this publication may be reproduced, stored in a retrieval system or transmitted, in any form or by any means, electronic, mechanical, photocopying, recording or otherwise, without the prior written permission of the publishers and copyright holders.

A record of this book is held at the British Library and the National Library of Australia.

ISBN 9781742578057

Managing Director: Fiona Schultz
Publisher: Alan Whiticker
Project Editor: Jessica McNamara
Designer: Peter Guo
Production Director: Olga Dementiev
Printer: Times Offset (M) Sdn Bhd

10 9 8 7 6 5 4 3 2 1

Keep up with New Holland Publishers on Facebook
www.facebook.com/NewHollandPublishers